Contents

WE SHOULD OFFER OURSELVES AND ALL THAT IS OURS TO GOD AND PRAY FOR ALL MEN

1

Lord, everything in heaven is yours, everything on earth. I desire to offer myself to you in willing surrender and to remain yours for ever. Lord, in singleness of heart I offer myself to you today, to be your servant for ever; this I do to shew my allegiance to you, as a sacrifice of everlasting praise. Take me, together with this holy sacrifice of your precious body, this offering that I make you today in the presence of the Angels who stand by unseen; may it further my salvation and that of all your people.

2

Lord, I offer you upon this altar of reconciliation all the sins and wrongdoing I have committed before you and your holy Angels, from the first day I had the power to sin up to this present time; burn and consume them all in the fire of your love; wipe out the stains of my sins; clean my conscience from every misdeed; give me back your grace, which through sin I have lost; grant me full pardon for all my offences, and mercifully receive me with the kiss of peace.

3

There is nothing I can do about my sins but humbly confess and bewail them, and cry without ceasing for your mercy. I beseech you, my God, mercifully hear me, as I stand here before you. All my sins are utterly abhorrent to me; I never want to commit them again. I grieve over them and shall grieve as long as I live; and I am ready to do penance for them and to atone for them as best I can. Do away with my sins, O my God, for thy holy name's sake do away with them; save my soul, which you have bought at the price of your precious blood. See, I entrust myself to your mercy, surrender myself into your hands. Deal with me according to your goodness, not according to my malice and sinfulness.

4

I offer you also all my good deeds, pitifully few and unfinished though they be. Do you amend and hallow them; make them pleasing and welcome to you, and ever raise them to greater heights; and bring me, slothful and useless specimen of humanity though I be, to a blessed and worthy end.

5

I offer you also all the devout yearnings of the faithful; the needs of my parents, my friends, my brothers and sisters and all who are dear to me; for those, too, who for love of you have shewn kindness to me or to others; for those who have desired or asked me to pray and say Mass for them and theirs, whether still living in the flesh or gone from this world. May they all be conscious of the approach of your helping grace, the support of your comfort, the withdrawal of pain; freed from all evils, may they duly give you thanks with solemn and joyful praise.

6

I offer you also my prayers and this appeasing sacrifice for those especially who have in any way hurt me, distressed me or spoken against me, or involved me in loss, or given me cause for grievance; for those, too, whom I have at any time distressed or troubled, pained or hindered from good, whether by word or deed, consciously or unawares. Do you forgive us all alike our sins and the hurt we do one another. Lord, take from our hearts all suspicion, ill-temper, anger and dissension and everything else that may be hurtful to charity and lessen brotherly love. Have mercy, Lord, have mercy on those who beg for your mercy; give your grace to those who stand in need of it; make us so to live that we may be worthy to enjoy your grace and make our way to life everlasting. Amen.

THE BODY OF CHRIST AND HOLY SCRIPTURE ARE MOST NECESSARY TO THE FAITHFUL SOUL

7

Jesus, my most sweet Lord, how great is the sweetness enjoyed by the faithful soul who feasts in your company and at your banquet; there no other food is set before her than you, her only beloved, one to be desired above all the desires of her heart. How sweet it would be for me, could I but weep before you, from the depth of the love within me, and with the devout Magdalen bathe your feet with my tears! But where is that devotion? Where that unstinted outpouring of holy tears? Surely, here before you and your holy Angels, my heart should be wholly aflame; I ought to be weeping for very joy, for here in this Sacrament I have you truly present, though hidden beneath another form.

8

Were I to gaze upon you in the blinding light of your Godhead, my eyes could not stand the sight; why, the whole world itself could not stay unmoved beneath the splendour, the glory of your majesty. It is out of consideration for my weakness that you veil yourself beneath this Sacrament. Here I truly hold, here I adore, him whom the Angels adore in heaven; I, as yet, by faith alone, they as he really is, with no veil between. I must be content with the light of true faith, walking by its rays until the dawning of the day of everlasting glory, when the shadows of outward seeming shall move away. But *when the time of fulfilment comes*,[11] there will be an end of using Sacraments; the Blessed in their heavenly glory have no need of the healing the Sacraments bestow. Joy without end is theirs, as in the presence of God they gaze upon his glory, face to face; transfigured from their own glory into that of the infinite Godhead, they taste the Word of God become flesh, as he was from the beginning and for ever remains.

9

When I recall these wonders to mind, I grow weary even of spiritual consolation; for so long as I may not see my Lord in his true glory, all that I see and hear in the world means nothing to me. You are my witness, O my God, that there is never a thing that can comfort me, never a creature that can bring me rest, save only you, my God, you upon whom I desire to gaze for ever. But this is not possible in this mortal life, and so I must have great patience and in all my desires submit myself to you. Those Saints of yours, Lord, who now rejoice with you in the kingdom of heaven, awaited the coming of your glory with faith and much patience while they lived on earth. What they believed, I too believe; what they hoped for, I hope for too; and through your grace I trust to come to that place where they have already arrived. Till that happens, I will walk in faith, strengthened by the examples of the Saints. I shall also have holy books to comfort me and to mirror the life I would lead; above all, your most holy body shall be my particular remedy and refuge.

10

Now I am deeply conscious that there are two things necessary for me in this life; without them, this same life and all its sorrows would be more than I could bear. Pent in the prison of my body, I confess my need for two things, food and light. It is for this that you have given me in my weakness your holy body, to be a refreshment for soul and body; and you have set your word as a lamp to guide my feet. Without these two I could not properly live; the word of God is the light of my soul, and your Sacrament is the bread of life. You might even call them two tables, set one on this side, one on that, in the treasury of holy Church. One table is that of the holy altar; on it is the holy bread, the precious body of Christ. The other table is that of God's law, whereon is holy teaching, instructing us in the true faith and leading us without stumbling even beyond the veil hiding the Holy of Holies. I thank you, Lord Jesus, for the table of holy teaching, spread for us by means of your servants the prophets and apostles and other holy teachers.

11

O Creator and Redeemer of men, I thank you for shewing the whole world your love for men in preparing a great feast. Here it is no longer the lamb of ancient times that you have set before us to eat, but your own most holy body and blood. At this holy banquet you gladden the faithful, who drink brimming draughts from the cup of salvation, that cup wherein are all the delights of heaven; the Angels, too, are our fellow guests, feasting with a joy even greater than ours.

12

How great and honourable is the office of those who are priests! They have been empowered to hallow with sacred words the Lord of majesty, to bless him with their lips, to hold him in their hands, to receive him with their own mouth and administer him to others. How frequently does the source of all purity enter into a priest! Then how pure should those hands of his be, how holy his body, how free from stain his heart. From the mouth of a priest, who so often receives the

Sacrament of Christ, no words should come forth but such as are holy, becoming and of benefit to others.

13

His eyes should be simple and chaste, for they often look upon the body of Christ, his hands pure and lifted up to heaven, for they often handle the Creator of heaven and earth. Priests in particular are addressed in those words of the Law, *You must be men set apart, as I am set apart, I, the Lord your God.*[12]

14

Almighty God, may we be helped by your grace; that we who have received the office of priesthood may be enabled to serve you worthily and devoutly in utter purity and with a good conscience. And if we cannot lead as sinless a life as we ought to, grant us nevertheless the grace to bewail the wrong we have done, and in the spirit of humility and with a resolve to choose the good, to serve you in future with greater fervour.

THE GRACE OF DEVOTION

15

O Lord my God, you are my total good; who am I, to dare speak to you? I am the least, the poorest of your servants, nothing but a wretched little worm, far poorer and more insignificant than I know or have the courage to say. Yet remember, Lord, that I am nothing, possess nothing, can do nothing. You alone are good, just and holy. You can do all things, grant all things, fill all things, leaving none but the sinner empty of your bounty. Remember your mercies; fill my heart with your grace, for it is not your wish that any of your works should be empty.

16

How can I bear this my life of sorrow, if you do not support me with your mercy and grace? Do not turn your face away from me; do not be long in coming to me; do not withdraw your consolation from me, or my soul will become like a land parched with drought. Lord, teach me to do what you want me to do. Teach me to live humbly and worthily in your presence. You are my wisdom; you know me as I really am, as you have done before the world was made, before by birth I came into this world.

WE MUST REST IN GOD ABOVE ALL HIS GIFTS AND FAVOURS

17

My soul, above all things and in all things you must always rest in the Lord, for he is the everlasting rest of the Saints. O sweetest, most loving Jesus, grant that I may rest in you above anything created; above all health and beauty, all honour and glory; above all power and dignity, all knowledge and cleverness; above all riches and abilities; above all joy and gladness, above all fame and praise; above all sweetness and consolation; above all hope and promise, above all merit and desire; above all gifts and presents you can give us or pour out upon us; above all happiness and rejoicing that the mind can grasp and feel; finally, above Angels and Archangels and above the whole host of heaven; above everything seen or unseen, above everything that is not you, my God.

18

O Lord my God, you are the sum of all good, surpassing all things; you alone are most high and most powerful; you alone are completely self-sufficient and perfect; you alone are most sweet and consoling. You alone are most beautiful and most loving, most noble and most glorious above all else; in you are found existing together in all their perfection all good things that now are or ever have been or ever will be. Thus it is that anything you give me apart from yourself, anything you reveal or promise me of yourself, is too little, too unsatisfying, for as yet I have not seen you, have not fully gained possession of you. My heart cannot find its true resting-place, cannot be wholly content, until it soars above all your gifts, all that you have created, and rests in you.

19

O Jesus Christ, my dearest spouse, my lover of stainless purity, ruler of the whole creation: who will give me wings of true freedom, that I may fly to you and in you take my rest? When will it be granted to me in full to have nothing to do but see how sweet you are, O Lord my God? When may I be wholly absorbed in you, that for very love of you I may be unaware of myself, may know only you, above all the ways we know through our senses, in a fashion not known to all? But now, how often I sigh, as I bear with grief my load of unhappiness! Many are the evils I meet with in this vale of sorrows; often they trouble me, sadden me, befog my path; often hinder and distract me, lure and entangle me, to prevent me from coming to you freely, from knowing the bliss of your embrace, which for the blessed spirits is an ever-present joy. Let my sighing touch your heart; in so many ways am I a lonely outcast upon earth!

20

O Jesus, brightness of the everlasting glory, comfort of the soul on its pilgrimage here, my lips beseech you without sound of words, my silence speaks to you. How much longer will my Lord delay his coming? I am but little and poor, but let him come to me and make me glad; let him stretch out his hand and rescue a poor wretch from all the troubles that fence him in. Ah, come, come! Without you, not a day is happy, not a single hour! You are my happiness; without you, there is no one to share my table. I am full of misery, something like a prisoner with his burden of fetters, until you cheer me with the light of your presence, give me back my freedom, and turn towards me the face of a friend.

Let others seek instead of you whatever takes their fancy; for me, there is nothing that gives me such joy, nor ever will be, but you, my God, my hope, my eternal salvation. I will not keep quiet, not cease to beg for your favour, until your grace returns and I hear your voice within me once more.

21

Lord, I called for you in my longing to enjoy your dear company; for your sake I am ready to give up all else. It was you who first moved me to seek you; bless you, Lord, for doing your servant this kindness in your unbounded mercy. What more can your servant say to you? He can only lie in utter abasement before you, ever conscious of his own sinfulness and unimportance. Yes, there is nothing to compare with you out of all the wonders of heaven and earth. All your works are good, all your judgements are true; your providence is at the helm of all creation. Let praise and glory be yours, then, O Wisdom of the Father; let my lips, my soul and the whole of creation together praise you and bless you.

ON RECALLING GOD's MANIFOLD BLESSINGS

22

Lord, open this heart of mine and place your law within it; teach me to walk by the road of your commandments. Grant that I may know what your will is; grant that my mind may dwell with great reverence and careful attention upon all your blessings, both those common to all men and those which are your gift to me; so may I be enabled to thank you in future as you deserve. Yet I know and confess that I am unable to praise and thank you as I ought, even for the very least of your favours. I am much less than all the blessings you have showered upon me; when I realize how infinitely high you are above your creation, my mind whirls at the thought of your greatness.

23

All qualities of soul and body that are ours, whatever we possess, inwardly or outwardly, naturally or supernaturally, come from your bounty; they shew us how bounteous you are, how loving, how good, you from whom we have received all these blessings. Some may have been given more, some less, but all alike come from you, and without you we could not have even the least of them. The man who has received a larger share cannot boast of it as being won by his own merit, cannot affect a superior attitude towards others or treat as dirt those less gifted than himself; the less a man attributes his good qualities to himself, the more humble and devout the thanks he gives to God for them, a greater man, a better man, is he. The man who ranks himself below all others and counts himself unworthy of God's favour is better fitted for receiving that favour in greater measure.

A PRAYER AGAINST EVIL THOUGHTS

24

O Lord my God, do not go far away from me; look upon me, my God, and help me, for swarming thoughts have broken out in rebellion against me, together with deep fears that harass my soul. How am I to pass through them without getting a wound? How am I to break my way through them?

Of old you said: *I will still lead you on your way, bending the pride of earth low before you*. I will open the gates of the prison, and shew you the mysteries of the secret places.

Lord, do as you have said: let all evil thoughts flee at the sight of you. This is my hope, my one comfort, that in all my troubles I can turn to you, trust you, call upon you from the depths of my being, and in patience wait for you to comfort me.

A PRAYER FOR LIGHT TO SHINE IN OUR MIND

25

O good Jesus, let the brightness of your inward light shine clearly within my mind; banish all darkness from the house of my heart. Fence in my many roving thoughts and crush the temptations that use such force against me. Fight on my side with all your strength and overcome those evil beasts, the fleshly lusts that lure me to wrong; so will your power bring peace, and the mighty sound of your praise ring out in that holy temple, a conscience free from stain. Give your commands to the winds and to the storms; bid the sea to be calm and the blustering wind not to blow, and there shall be a great stillness.

26

Send forth your light and your truth to shine upon the earth; I myself am but earth, empty and waste, until you shed your light upon me. Pour down your grace from above; soak my heart with the rain of heaven; bring me streams of devotion to water the face of this earth, to make it bear good and perfect fruit. Take from my mind the load of sin that weighs so heavily upon it, and fix all my desires upon the things of heaven, so that, once I have tasted the sweetness of that joy above, I may be loth to let my thoughts dwell on the things of earth.

27

Catch hold of me and drag me away from the comfort to be found in things created, a comfort that cannot last; for there is nothing in all creation that can fully slake my longings, fully give me comfort. Bind me to you with a bond of love that cannot be broken; for you alone are all-in-all for a loving heart, and without you everything else is but pitiful trash.

ON THE EXCELLENCE OF A FREE MIND, THE REWARD OF HUMBLE PRAYER RATHER THAN OF READING

28

Lord, it is the business of a man of perfect life never to loosen the bonds that bind his heart to heavenly things; to make his way through a crowd of troubles as if he had no trouble at all, not like someone too stupid to be alive to his plight but in the privileged possession of a free mind that clings to nothing in creation with ill-regulated affection.

29

O most loving God, I beg you to keep me from the cares of this life, so that I may not become too closely involved in them; from the many needs of the body, for fear of the snares of pleasure; from everything that blocks the way my soul would go, that I may not be overwhelmed by my troubles and become downcast. I do not ask to be kept from those things that are pursued so whole-heartedly by the frivolous and the worldly, but from those miseries which weigh so heavily, so painfully, upon the soul of your servant, who shares in the curse pronounced on mortal man in general, miseries that hold him back from entering into spiritual freedom as often as he would like to.

30

O my God, you who are sweetness surpassing all speech, turn sour for me the taste of any bodily comfort that draws me away from the love of eternal things, enticing me, to my hurt, by the sight of some pleasure to be enjoyed in this present life. Do not let them overcome me, my God, do not let them overcome me, this flesh and blood of mine; let me not be deceived by the world and its fleeting glory; do not let the Devil and his wiles trip me by the heels. Give me strength to resist, patience to hold out, steadfastness to keep going until the end. Give me the sweet balm of your spirit instead of all the delights of the world; empty my heart of fleshly love and fill it instead with the love of your name.

31

To a fervent spirit, having to make use of food, drink, clothing and other things to keep the body going is a burden; grant that I may be sparing in my use of such bodily comforts and not over-anxious to enjoy them. It is not right to dispense with them entirely; we have to make provision for the needs of our nature; but your holy law forbids us to seek for unnecessary luxuries. Otherwise, if we did, the flesh would rise in revolt against the spirit. In all these matters, I pray that I may be guided and directed by your hand, so as to avoid extravagance.

A PRAYER FOR A CLEAN HEART AND HEAVENLY WISDOM

32

O God, strengthen me by the grace of your Holy Spirit. Make firm within me my efforts to be holy; empty my heart of all unnecessary worry and anxiety, and do not let it be carried away by the desire of anything whatsoever, whether worth the having or otherwise. Make me see that all things are passing away, and that I, too, must one day follow them; for there is nothing beneath the sun that lasts for ever, and everything here is *but frustration and lost labour, all of it.*[27] He is a wise man whose thoughts run thus.

33

Lord, give me your heavenly wisdom, that I may learn to seek you and find you above all things else, to love and understand you more than anything; let me see all other things as they are, in the way your wisdom has disposed them. Give me the prudence to keep away from those who flatter me, the patience to bear with those who oppose me. This is wisdom indeed, to refuse to be swayed by every gust of speech from the mouths of men, and not to give ear to those Siren voices that lure a man so sweetly to his doom. Following such a course, we advance fearlessly along the road we have begun to tread.

HOW WE SHOULD CALL ON GOD AND BLESS HIM WHEN TROUBLE THREATENS

34

Lord, may your name be blessed for ever; it is by your will that this trouble and temptation have come upon me. I cannot get out of it, but I must come to you for protection, that you may help me and make it turn out for my good. Lord, I am in trouble at the moment; there is no peace in my heart, but I am much disturbed by this affliction now pressing on me. What can I say now, my beloved Father? I am trapped in a tight place. *Save me from undergoing this hour of trial.*[28] Yet that is why I have come to this hour, to bring you the glory of setting me free from this pit of humiliation. Please rescue me, Lord; what can I do, resourceless as I am? Without you, where shall I go? Lord, give me patience, this time also. Help me, my God, and I shall have no fear, no matter how heavy the load I must bear.

35

What shall I say now in the midst of my distress? Lord, may your will be done. I have richly deserved trouble and oppression. I must certainly endure it—patiently, I hope—until the storm blows over and things get better. Your hand is almighty, and has the power to take even this temptation away from me and soften its violence, so that I may not completely give way before it; many a time in the past you have done that for me, my God in your mercy towards me. To me, such a change seems unlikely; that only makes it easier, O God most high, for you to bring it about and lighten my burden.

GOD, ABOVE ALL THINGS AND IN ALL THINGS, IS THE DELIGHT OF THE LOVING HEART

36

My God, my all, you are here; what more can I wish for, what greater happiness can I desire?

O sweet and delightful word! But sweet only to those who love the Word, not to those who love the world and all that is in the world. My God, my all! To one who understands, that is enough said; to one who loves, it is something to be said over and over again, each time with joy. When you are present, there is joy in everything; when you are not, all things are distasteful. You set the heart at rest, you bring great peace and joy and mirth. You make us think well of all and praise you in all. There is nothing that can please us for long without you; but if it is to be enjoyable and to our taste, your grace must be within it, it needs to be flavoured with the spice of your wisdom.

37

When a man finds delight in you, what is there he will not find delight in? When a man takes no delight in you, what will be able to give him pleasure? But those who are wise in a worldly way, those who have the wisdom of the sensualist, are lacking in your wisdom; the former have nothing but utter emptiness, the latter find death. But those who by scorning worldly ways and chastening their bodily desires follow your own path, they are the really wise men; they have passed from empty folly to truth, from the flesh to the spirit. For such as these, God is their keenest delight: if they *do* find any good in creatures, they make it an additional reason for praising their Maker. But oh! how different, how immeasurably different, is the delight to be found in the Creator and that in things created; how little does eternity resemble time, or uncreated Light the borrowed brightness of creation!

38

O light unending, O light surpassing all that shines in your creation, send down from on high the lightning-stroke of your dazzling brilliance, to pierce and free from darkness the most secret depths of my heart! Seize my spirit and all its powers; give it your purity, your gladness, your brightness, your life, that it may cling to you in an ecstasy of joy. Ah, when will it come, that blissful and longed-for hour, when the joy of your presence shall brim to overflowing the depths of my desire, and you be my all in all? Until you grant me that, my joy cannot be full. Still does the man I was—I grieve to say it—stir to life within me; he is not completely nailed to the cross, not finally and utterly dead. Still do his lusts make violent war against the spirit, making my heart the battle-ground of civil war, so that the kingdom of my soul may not be at peace.

39

Arise and help me, my God, you who govern the might of the sea and calm the turbulent waves! Scatter the nations that delight in war; let that power of yours crush them. Shew them, I beg you, what mighty things you can do, and let them see the glorious power that lies in your hand; but for you, O Lord my God, I have no hope, no place where I may find shelter.

DIVINE LOVE

40

Father in heaven, Father of Jesus Christ my Lord, I bless you for deigning to remember me and my poverty. Father of mercies, God of all comfort, I thank you for refreshing me with your comfort, little though I deserve any comfort at all. To you and your only-begotten Son, together with the Holy Ghost, the Comforter, I give blessing and glory always, both now and for ages without end. Ah, Lord God, you the holy one, you my lover, when you come into my heart, the whole of my inmost being will leap with joy. You are my glory, the comfort of my heart; my stronghold and my refuge in my hour of peril.

41

As yet I am but weak in love, unsure in virtue; that is why I need your support, your comfort. So come to me, come to me often and teach me what is in your holy laws. Set me free from evil passions; heal my heart of all its ill-regulated affections; so that, whole and pure in my inmost being, I may become ready to love, strong to endure suffering, steadfast to persevere.

42

A mighty force it is, this thing love, mighty and altogether good; alone it takes the weight from every burden, alone it bears evenly the uneven load. It bears a burden as if no burden were there, makes the bitter things of life sweet and good to taste. To love Jesus is a wondrous thing; it urges men on to mighty deeds, stirs up in them the desire for a life ever more holy. Love must be ever mounting on high, unfettered by things below; love would ever be free, a stranger to every worldly desire, fearful lest its inward vision grow clouded, lest some worldly gain should encumber its advance, some worldly misfortune bring it headlong down. There is nothing sweeter than love, nothing stronger, nothing higher, nothing wider, nothing fuller, nothing better in heaven or earth; for love is born of God, and only in God, above all that he has created, can it find rest.

43

A man in love treads on air; he runs for very joy. He is a free man; nothing can hold him back. He gives all for all, finding his rest in one who is high above all else, the source and origin of all that is good. For gifts he has no regard, but turns to him who is their giver, who is above all good gifts. Love often knows no limits; its impetuous fire leaps across every boundary. Love feels no burden, makes light of toil, strives for things beyond its strength. Love never tries to make out that anything is impossible; everything, in the eyes of love, is both possible and lawful. Love, then, can do everything; many a task there is that love can fulfil and many a wish it can make effective, where the man who does not love is powerless and fails.

44

Love is ever on the watch; it rests, but does not slumber, is wearied but not spent, alarmed but not dismayed; like a living flame, a blazing torch, it shoots upward, fearlessly passing through aught that bars its path. If anyone has this love, he will know what I mean. A loud cry in the ears of God is that burning love for him in the soul which says: "My God, my love, you are all mine and I all yours."

45

Let my love know no bounds; let me learn to taste with the lips of my inmost being how sweet it is to love, to melt in love's fire, to float on the waves of love! Let love keep hold of me, as in unwonted fervour and wonder I rise above my usual self. Let me sing the song of love and follow you, my Beloved, to high heaven; let my soul grow faint in praising you, rejoicing in your love. Let me love you more than myself, love myself only for your sake; let me love in you all who truly love you—that is the bidding of the law of love, that law whose light streams forth from you.

46

Love is swift, pure, dutiful, pleasant and agreeable; it is strong, patient, faithful, prudent, long-suffering, manly, never seeking its own advantage. For when anyone seeks that, he falls away from love. Love is wary, humble and upright; it is not soft, not unstable, not intent on empty trifles; it is sober, chaste, steadfast, keeping due watch on all the senses. Love is submissive and obedient to those in authority, mean and contemptible in its own regard. To God it is ever devout and thankful, ever trusting and hoping in him even when it cannot taste his sweetness; for there is no living a life of love without sorrow.

47

The man who is not ready to endure everything and stand fast by the will of his Beloved does not deserve to be called a lover; a lover should be glad to welcome all sorts of hardship and bitterness for the sake of his Beloved, and never let himself turn away from him when things go against him.

A MAN HAS NO GOODNESS OF HIS OWN, AND NOTHING TO BOAST OF

48

What is man that you should remember him? What is Adam's breed, that it should claim your care?[40] What has man done, to deserve the gift of your grace? If you abandon me, Lord, how can I complain? If you don't answer my prayer, what right have I to object? But this is something I can think and say, and it will be true: "Lord, I am nothing, can do nothing; I have no goodness of my own, in nothing do I reach perfection, but have a constant tendency towards nothingness. Unless you help me and work upon my heart I become completely lukewarm and lax."

49

But you, Lord, are always the same and remain so for ever; always good and just and holy, acting always with goodness, justice and holiness, and arranging all things in your wisdom. As for me, I tend to slip back rather than go forward; never do I stay for long in any one state; and I must pass through the seven ages of man, with all their attendant changes. And yet, the moment it pleases you to stretch out your helping hand, I am at once all the better for it; for you alone, without any help from man, can come to my assistance, so strengthening me, that I may no longer direct my gaze this way and that at one thing or another, but turn my heart to you alone, and there find rest.

50

If only I could do without all comfort that comes from man, either to further my devotion or because I needs must seek you, seeing there is no man who can comfort me! I might well then hope for your grace, and rejoice at being given once more your gift of comfort.

51

Every time things go well with me, I thank you, because it all comes from you. In your sight I am but emptiness and nothing, a strengthless, unstable man, so what have I got to be proud of? Why do I long for people to think well of me? Of me, of nothing? Folly can go no further. Such groundless conceit is indeed a canker of the soul and the height of foolishness; it lures a man away from true glory and strips him bare of heavenly grace. So long as a man is foolishly pleased with himself, to you he is only displeasing; so long as he covets the good opinion of men, he is depriving himself of true virtue.

52

The real way to take pride and be filled with holy joy is to take pride not in oneself but in you, to rejoice in your name, not in one's own strength, and to find no pleasure in anything created except for your sake. May your name be praised, not mine; your works commended, not mine; may your holy name be blessed, but let me have no share in the praises of men. You are my pride and glory, the joy of my heart. In you I will take pride and rejoice the livelong day; in myself I will take no pride, except perhaps in my own weaknesses.

53

Let the Jews seek the kind of glory that men give one another; the glory I shall seek is that which is given by God alone. All human glory, all this world's honours, all high positions on earth, look meaningless and silly when set beside your everlasting glory. O blessed Trinity, my God, my truth, my mercy, to you alone belong praise, honour, power and glory, through endless ages and ages.

ON PUTTING OUR TRUST IN GOD WHEN OTHERS MAKE STINGING REMARKS

54

Lord God, you who as a judge are just, patient and strong, you who know the frailty and crookedness of men, I ask you to be my strength, that I may put complete trust in you; my conscience by itself is not enough. You know what I do not; that should have made me humble myself whenever I was reprimanded, made me meekly bear the reproof. Be merciful; forgive me for all the times I have failed to act in that way; give me grace once more to endure things for longer than I have. The flood of your mercy will better avail me if I would be pardoned, than my protestation of innocence will be echoed by my inmost conscience. I may not be conscious of any fault, but that is no reason for complacency; if you withhold your mercy, *what man is there living that can stand guiltless in your presence*?

ON THE DAY OF ETERNITY AND THE TROUBLES OF THIS LIFE

55

How happy are those who dwell for ever in the city that is above! How bright is the day of eternity! It is a day upon which night casts no shadow, but one for ever lit by the very Truth; a day for ever happy, for ever safe, a day that never changes into the contrary. Oh, how I wish that day had already dawned, and all these things of time come to an end! For the Saints, that day is already shining, bright with a radiance that goes on and on; for us who are still making our earthly pilgrimage, it shines only from a distance; we can see its reflection, so to speak, only in a looking-glass.

56

Those who are townsmen of the heavenly city know how joyful the day is there; we, the outcast children of Eve, know how bitter and wearisome the day can be on earth. Yes, the days of time are few and evil indeed, full of sorrow and trouble. Here man is befouled by many sins, enmeshed in many passions, brushed close by many fears. He is tormented by many cares, dragged this way and that by many strange sights, entangled in many kinds of folly. Many an error surrounds him, many a hard task leaves him exhausted; he is burdened with temptations, enfeebled by pleasures, racked with want.

57

Oh, when will these evils come to an end? When shall I be freed from the wretched slavery of sin? Lord, when shall I think only of you, find in you my full measure of gladness? When shall I be really free, with nothing to hinder me, nothing to drag me down in mind or body? When will there be lasting peace, peace for ever safe and never to be disturbed, peace both within and without, peace that in every way stands unchanged? Good Jesus, when shall I stand in your sight and see you? When shall I gaze upon the glory of your kingdom? When will you be all in all to me? Oh, when shall I be in that kingdom of yours which you have made ready from all time for those you love? Here I have been left behind in enemy territory, a poor outcast in a land where every day there is fighting, every day disasters most dire.

58

Comfort me in this my exile; assuage my grief; it is to you that I sigh with all my longing. Whatever this world can offer me by way of comfort is nothing but a burden to me; I long for the bliss of your close company, but I am unable to reach so far. I yearn to hold fast to heavenly things, but I am weighed down by the things of the time, by passions far from dead. With my mind I long to rise superior to all these things, but my body compels me to be their unwilling slave. Thus it comes about that I, poor piece of humanity, am the theatre of civil war, a burden to myself, with the spirit trying to soar aloft, and the body endeavouring to stay below.

59

What I go through inwardly, when my mind is groping its way towards the things of heaven, and, during my very prayer, a crowd of worldly thoughts comes rushing into my head! Do not go far away from me, my God, do not turn away in anger from this servant of yours. Dazzle them with the stroke of your lightning, and scatter them; shoot forth your arrows, and so put to rout all the drifting thoughts sent by my enemy. Gather my senses together and fix them on yourself; make me forget all that is in the world; give me the power to hurl back and to scorn all mental pictures of evil deeds. Come to my help, O everlasting Truth, so that no empty folly may sway my heart. O heavenly sweetness, come to me, and all that is foul will flee at sight of you. Forgive me, also, and in your mercy grant me pardon for all the times I think of anything besides you in time of prayer; because, to confess the truth, I am usually in a state of great distraction. Often enough I am not where my body is, whether standing or sitting, but wherever my thoughts carry me to. Wherever my thoughts are, there am I; and my thoughts are usually with the things I love. What comes most readily to mind is something naturally pleasant or found by experience to be agreeable.

60

It was this that made you, the very Truth, say plainly: *Where your treasure-house is, there your heart is too.*[49] If I love heaven, I readily think of heavenly things; if I love the world, I share the world's gladness when it rejoices, and am sad when it is thwarted. If I love the body, I often picture to myself bodily delights; if I love the spirit, I love thinking about spiritual matters. Whatever it is that I like best, those are the things I love talking and hearing about; and I bring home mental pictures of them with me from the world outside. But happy is the man who for your sake, Lord, has, so to speak, given all things created notice to quit; the man who gets tough with nature and crucifies the lusts of his body with the burning desires of his spirit. Such a man has put his conscience at rest and can offer you unblemished prayer; by closing the door on earthly interests, both in his life and in his heart, he is worthy to mingle with the choirs of Angels.

HOW A MAN OUGHT TO PUT HIMSELF IN GOD'S HANDS IN TIME OF TROUBLE

61

Lord God, holy Father, may you be blessed both now and for ever; whatever happens comes about because you wish it so; and what you do is good. I am your servant; let me rejoice not in myself or in any other, but in you, because you alone are my real happiness; you are my hope and my crown, Lord, my joy and my honour. What does this servant of yours possess that he has not received from you, and that through no merit of his own? Everything is yours, both what you have given and what you have made. *Ever since youth, misery and mortal sickness have been my lot*;[50] often enough I am so sad at heart that my eyes fill with tears, and sometimes my soul is in turmoil because of the strong feelings that oppress it.

62

I long for the joy of your peace, praying hard for the peace enjoyed by your children who are allowed by you to roam the shining pastures of your consolation. If you give me this peace, if you flood my heart with holy joy, my soul will burst into joyful song and devote itself to praising you; but if you withdraw from me, as you do so often, I shall be unable to run on the road of your commandments. Instead, on bended knees I shall beat my breast, because my life is no longer what it was yesterday and the day before, when your lantern gleamed above my head, and I found in the shelter of your wings a refuge from the temptations that assailed me.

63

Father of all justice, you who are ever to be praised, the hour has come for the testing of this servant of yours. Father to whom all love is due, it is right that your servant should suffer something on this occasion for your sake. Father to whom we owe unceasing worship, the time has come which you foresaw from all eternity would meet me, the time for your servant to fall low for a while in the eyes of the world, though in your sight his inner life remains ever as it was. For a short time he must be scoffed at, humiliated and brought low in the eyes of men, tormented by the vehemence of his feelings and by weakness, that with you he may rise again in the dawn of a new day, and in heaven be clothed with glory. Holy Father, that is the way you have decreed it should happen, the way you have willed it; what has happened has happened by your command.

64

That is the way you shew favour to any friend of yours: you let him suffer and meet with trouble in this world, for love of you; the number of times this shall happen, and the instrument of his affliction, are determined by your permission, for nothing on earth takes place that has not been planned by you, foreseen by you; nothing happens by chance. *It was in mercy you did chasten me, schooling me to your obedience*;[51] I will renounce all elation of heart, all presumption. It is good for me to have known disgrace; let it make me seek you, rather than men, to bring me comfort. Another lesson I have learned from this experience, that of standing in dread of your unsearchable judgement; because you afflict the good along with the wicked, yet not without being fair and just in your judgement.

65

Thank you for not sparing my evildoing, but for chastising me instead with the lash of bitter grief, afflicting me with sorrows and sending me troubles both inward and outward. There is nothing can comfort me, of everything beneath the heavens, but you alone, my Lord and my God; you are the heavenly healer, the Lord of life and death, *who brings men to the grave and back from the grave;*[52] your tender care is above me; your very rod teaches me a lesson.

66

See, my beloved Father, I am in your hands; I bend low to take the blows of your chastening rod. Strike me where you will, across the back, across the neck, and make me bring my crooked ways in line with your will. Make a loving and humble pupil of me, as you have so often made others, one who will take a step only at a sign from you. To you, Lord, I offer for your correction both myself and all that is mine; it is better to be punished here than in the world to come. You know all that is, and every single part of that all; for you no one's conscience has any secrets. You know the future before it comes along; and you have no need of anyone to tell you what is happening on earth. You know what I need if I am to make any progress, know how efficient much trouble can be in scrubbing away the rust of my sins. Make me long to do what pleases you best, and do not scorn my sinful life, that no one knows better or more clearly than you alone.

67

Lord, grant that I may know what I ought to know, love what I ought to love, praise what best pleases you, value what you deem precious, condemn whatever in your eyes seems filthy. Let me not judge things by outward appearances or form my opinions on the hearsay of those who know but little; give me that true judgement which can form a correct opinion on matters both of the world we see and that other world of the spirit; and let me above all else ever seek what best pleases your will.

68

Men's senses often lead them astray when it comes to deciding any matter; there are others led astray, too, by loving only what they can see, I mean the lovers of this world. What does a man gain from being held in high repute by someone else? When one man praises another, it is a case of one hypocrite deceiving his fellow hypocrite, the blind cheating the blind, the weak the weak; and so meaningless the praise is, it's really more of a disgrace to its recipient than anything else. "What every man is in your sight, Lord, that is what he is, and nothing more"; it was the humble St. Francis who said that.

A MAN OUGHT TO THINK HE DESERVES NOT CONSOLATION BUT PUNISHMENT

69

Lord, I am unworthy of your comfort, and indeed of any spiritual approach of yours. When you leave me poor and forsaken, I am getting no more than my due. If I could shed as many tears as there are drops in the sea, I should still be unworthy of consolation. No, all I deserve is whipping and punishment, for many is the time I have offended you—gravely, too—and many the evil deeds I have done. So, looking at things as they really are, I do not deserve the least bit of comfort. But you are the God of mercy, the God of pity; it is not your will that what you have made should perish. You would shew the riches of your loving kindness, pouring them into empty vessels which await your mercy; and therefore you stoop from heaven to console this servant of yours beyond anything he could have deserved, and in a way surpassing human ken; because your consolation is a very different thing from the empty mouthings of men.

70

What have I done, Lord, for you to bring me any comfort from heaven? I have never done any good, as far as I know, but have always been prone to sin and slow to amend. That is the truth, and I cannot deny it; if I said anything else, you would confront me, and there would be no one to defend me. What have I deserved for my sins but hell and everlasting fire? All I deserve, frankly speaking, is to be scoffed at and scorned; I am not good enough to be counted among your devoted servants. This is going to make painful hearing for me, but for truth's sake I will accuse myself of my sins, in the hope that I may deserve the more readily to win your merciful forgiveness.

71

Yes, I am guilty, one mass of shame; what am I to say? Not a word will come; all I can say is, "I have sinned, Lord, I have sinned; have mercy on me and pardon me". *For a little leave me to myself, to find some comfort in my misery. Soon I must go to a land whence there is no returning, a land of darkness, death's shadow over it.*[54] Why are you so insistent in asking a poor, guilty sinner to repent and humble himself for the wrong he has done? It is because from real repentance and humbleness of heart is born the hope of pardon; the conscience that was troubled is restored to God's favour, the grace that has been lost is returned, and man is shielded from the wrath to come. God and the penitent soul run to meet each other with a holy kiss.

72

Humble repentance for sin is a welcome sacrifice to you, Lord; it is far more fragrant in your sight than the smoke of burned incense. It is also the sweet ointment which you once desired to have poured over your feet; for you have never despised a contrite and humble heart. It is there that we can find a place of shelter from the face of our raging enemy; it is there that whatever has somehow got broken is mended, whatever has been soiled washed clean again.

ON THE CORRUPTION OF NATURE, AND THE POWER OF GOD'S GRACE

73

O Lord my God, you have made me in your own image and likeness; grant me this grace, which, as you have shewn, is so great a one, so necessary if I am to be saved: the grace of overcoming my own evil propensities, which drag me into sin and the loss of my soul. I am aware in my body of the authority of sin, opposing the authority of my mind, leading me away in bondage to give in to my sensual inclinations in many a way. I cannot resist its fierce promptings unless your holy grace comes to my rescue, filling my heart with its fiery glow.

74

Yes, I need your grace, and a lot of it at that, if I am to overcome nature, always bent on evil from youth upwards. It was through Adam, the first man, that it fell and was spoiled by sin; and the penalty for that blemish upon humanity has come down upon all men. That very nature which, as made by you, was good and upright, now stands for something vicious, for the weakness of a nature given over to corruption; that is because its instincts, left to themselves, drag the man in whom it has found towards evil and base desires. What little strength has remained is like a little spark hidden among ashes. This is natural reason itself, which, though shut in by intense darkness, can still tell good from evil, still separate truth from falsehood. Yet it is powerless to carry out all it approves of, and now no longer possesses the full light of truth nor the wholesome affections it once had.

75

Thus it comes about, my God, that I take pleasure in your law as far as my inner self is concerned: I know that what you command will be good, just and holy, bidding me shun any kind of evil and sin. Yet with my body I serve the powers of evildoing, by listening to my sensual feelings rather than to reason. Hence, though the will to do good is within me, I cannot find the strength to obey it. Another result is that, although I am always making good resolutions, yet through lack of grace to help my weakness, I recoil in failure at the least sign of opposition. Again, I know the way of perfection and can see perfectly clearly how I ought to behave; but the weight of my own corruption lies heavy on me, and I cannot rise to heights of greater perfection.

76

Lord, your grace is absolutely necessary for me for starting off some good act, for improving it, for making it perfect. Without it I can do nothing; in you, and with the support of your grace, I can do anything. Ah yes, grace is something from heaven; without it, our own merits are nothing, our natural gifts of no account whatever. Skill, wealth, beauty, courage, ability, eloquence—all these have no value in your eyes, Lord, unless grace goes with them. The gifts of nature are shared by good and bad alike, whereas grace, or love, is given especially to God's chosen; those who bear its mark are thought worthy of eternal life. This grace holds so high a position that not even the gift of prophecy, nor the working of miracles, nor the highest reaches of mystical vision are worth anything apart from it. Why, not even faith, hope and the other virtues are acceptable to you without love and grace.

77

It is indeed a blessed thing, grace; it makes the poor in spirit rich in virtues, the man of many riches humble of heart. Ah, come, come down to me and fill me with your comfort, like dew at morning, if you would not have my soul faint with weariness and spiritual drought! Lord, I beg that I may find favour in your sight; your favour, your grace, is enough for me, even if I fail to obtain those other things that nature thirsts for. No matter how many trials and troubles afflict me, I will fear no evil, so long as your grace is with me; it is my strength, bringing me counsel and help, mightier than all my enemies, wiser than all who are wise.

78

It is your grace that teaches us the truth, tells us what rule of life to follow, brings light to our hearts and comfort in our troubles; it drives away sadness, washes away fear, feeds our devotion and moves us to tears of repentance. Without it, what am I but a tree without rain, a useless bit of timber fit only to be thrown out? So let your grace, Lord, always go in front of me and behind me, to keep me constantly in mind of good deeds to be done; through Jesus Christ, your Son. Amen.

ALL OUR HOPE AND TRUST MUST BE PLACED IN GOD ALONE

79

Lord, what can I rely on in this life? What is my greatest comfort of all that can be seen under heaven? Is it not you, my Lord and my God, you whose mercy is beyond reckoning? Where have things gone well with me, with you not there? And when could things have gone badly for me, with you at my side? I had rather be poor for your sake than rich without you. I would choose to roam the world with you beside me than possess heaven and not you; but heaven is where you are, and where you are not—that is what death is, and hell. It is for you that I long; it is this longing that constrains me to sigh for you, to call out to you, to beg you for help. Finally, there is no one I can trust unreservedly, no one who in my need will help me at just the right moment, but you alone, my God. You are my hope, my trust, my comfort, always standing by me whatever happens.

80

All men seek their own advantage; all *your* scheming, Lord, is for my salvation, my betterment. Under your hands, everything turns out to be for my good. You may let me in for all sorts of trials and troubles, but you arrange for things to happen in that way only for my own good. Testing them in all sorts of fashions is a way you have of dealing with those whom you love; so when you test me like that I ought to love you and praise you just as much as if you were filling me with your heavenly consolation.

81

It is in you, then, Lord God, that I put all my hope, to you that I run for protection; in your hands I put all my troubles and misery. If I look at anything apart from you for help, I find nothing but uncertainty and doubtful stability. Having a lot of friends won't help me, having influential people to back me won't further my cause. If I ask the wise for advice, they can give me no answer I can act on; there can be no comfort for me in the books of the learned. No precious substance can buy my freedom, no private paradise afford me shelter. No, Lord, none of these can help me unless you yourself stand by me, helping me, strengthening and comforting me, instructing and keeping watch over me.

82

When you are not with me, everything that seems likely to bring me peace and happiness means nothing to me; things like that don't really make me happy. You are the goal for which all good men are striving; you are the highest peak of all that has life, the lowest deep that underlies all speech. Nothing is so great a comfort to your servants as to trust in you above all else. It is to you, my God, I raise my eyes, in you, O Father of mercies, that I place my trust. Bless and make holy this soul of mine with your heavenly blessing; so let it become a place sacred enough for you to dwell in it, a place where your eternal glory may stay for ever. Let nothing be found in this temple of your greatness on which your royal glance might light with disfavour. In the immensity of your goodness, the unmeasured stores of your mercy, look upon me and listen to the prayer of this poor servant of yours, so far from home here in the land of the shadow of death. Guard and keep the soul of this least of your servants amid the many dangers of this uncertain life. Give me your grace for my companion, and guide me along the path of peace, until I reach my true country, the land of unending light. Amen.

ON BURNING LOVE AND EAGER LONGING TO RECEIVE CHRIST

83

With all my devotion, Lord, with burning love, with all the fervent longing of my heart, I desire to receive you, as many Saints and devout folk have longed to receive you in Communion, people who were especially pleasing to you because their lives were holy, people in whom the fire of devotion blazed the highest. O my God, my everlasting love, my all-embracing good, my bliss without end, with irresistible longing I desire to receive you, with the fittest reverence that ever any Saint had or could feel.

84

Unworthy though I am to have such feelings of devotion as theirs, I offer you nonetheless my heart's whole love, as if I alone were filled by all those fiery longings of theirs for which I yearn so much. Nevertheless, whatever a devout soul can imagine or desire, that do I offer you, that do I make you a gift of, with the deepest reverence, the love of my inmost self. Nothing do I choose to keep back for myself, but freely and with all my heart I make an offering to you of myself and all that is mine. O Lord my God, my Creator, my Redeemer, I desire to receive you this day with affection, reverence, praise and honour, with that thankfulness, fitness and love, with that faith, hope and purity with which your most holy Mother, the glorious Virgin Mary, desired and received you, when the Angel brought her the glad news of the mystery of the incarnation, and she in lowly reverence replied: *Behold the handmaid of the Lord; let it be unto me according to thy word.*

85

Of old that blessed forerunner of yours, John the Baptist, highest among the Saints, filled with gladness at your presence, leaped for joy of the Holy Spirit while still in the shelter of his mother's womb. In after years, when he saw Jesus walking among men, in utter abasement he said with loving devotion: *The bridegroom's friend, who stands by and listens to him, rejoices too, rejoices at hearing the bridegroom's voice.*[17] So it is with me: I long to be afire with great and holy desires, and with all my heart to offer you myself. It is for this reason that I offer and lay before you the worship you receive from all devout hearts—their outbursts of joyous praise, their burning affection, their ecstasies, their spiritual insight, their heavenly visions; to these I add all the virtues, all the praises, that ever have been or will be offered to you in heaven or upon earth. I offer them for myself and for all for whom I have been asked to pray, that you may be given by all men that praise which is your due, and glory that has no end.

86

O Lord my God, accept these my prayers, this my desire that the praises men give you should have no limit, the times they bless you surpass all reckoning; for these are your lawful due, you whose greatness is such that it outsoars all human speech. So do I pray to you, so do I wish to pray each day, each moment of time; and with loving entreaty I beg and beseech all spirits in heaven and all your faithful on earth to join with me in giving you the praise and thanksgiving that are yours by right.

87

May all peoples, tribes and tongues give praise to you; may they extol that holy, that honey-sweet name of yours with cries of joyful praise and burning devotion; and may all who worshipfully and devoutly celebrate this great Sacrament of yours and receive it with unfailing faith, deserve to find grace and mercy at your hands; and may they by their entreaties win your pardon for me and my sins; and when they have gained the devotion they hoped for, gained that union with yourself which is to bring them joy, and, greatly consoled and wonderfully refreshed, have left your sacred, your heavenly table, may they in kindness remember me and my poverty.

THE DEVOUT SOUL SHOULD LONG WITH HEARTFELT DESIRE FOR UNION WITH CHRIST IN THE BLESSED SACRAMENT

88

If only, Lord, I might find you by yourself and lay bare to you all that is in my heart! Then I could enjoy your company, as my soul desires; then no one would scorn me, nothing created would trouble me or concern me; you alone would speak to me, as a lover does to his beloved, as a friend makes cheer with his friend. This is what I pray for, long for: to be made wholly one with you, to withdraw my heart from all created things, and through Holy Communion and frequent saying of Mass to learn more and more to delight in heavenly and eternal things. Ah, Lord God, when shall I be completely one with you, completely absorbed in you, utterly forgetful of myself? You in me and I in you; grant that we may remain in one for ever.

89

You are indeed *my sweetheart. Among ten thousand you shall know him*; in you my soul delights to make her home all the days of my life. You are he who brings me peace; in you is peace untroubled, rest unfeigned. Apart from you there is only toil and trouble and boundless grief. *Truly you are a God of hidden ways*;[13] no dealings do you have with the godless, but to lowly and simple folk you speak your heart. Lord, how sweet is your spirit! To shew your loving-kindness towards your children, you deign to refresh them with that most sweet bread that comes down from heaven. How true it is that *no other nation is so great; no other nation has gods that draw near to it, as our God draws near to*[14] all his faithful. To comfort them every day, to raise their hearts daily to heaven, you give yourself to be their food and their delight.

90

What other people is so honoured as the Christian people? What creature under heaven is so beloved as a devout soul into whom God finds entrance, to nourish her with his glorious body? It is a grace that beggars speech, a stooping to our lowliness that fills us with wonder; a love beyond all measure, bestowed on mankind alone. But what return shall I make to the Lord for this grace, this love so high above other loves? No gift more welcome can I make him than to make over to him the whole of my heart, to be made one with his in the closest of unions. My whole inner being will be filled with joy when my soul is perfectly united to God. He will say to me then: “If you wish to be with me, I wish to be with you”. And I shall answer him thus: “Stay with me, Lord, I beg you; willingly will I stay with you”. This is the sum of my desires, that my heart should be united to you.

ON THE GREAT GOODNESS AND LOVE SHEWN BY GOD TO MAN IN THIS SACRAMENT

91

Trusting in your goodness, Lord, in your great mercy, I come in my sickness to him who can make me well; hungered and athirst, I come to the fountain of life, a beggar to the King of Heaven, a servant to his Lord, a creature to his Creator, one lonely and sad to him who loves and consoles me. But what have I done to deserve that you should come to me? Who am I, that you should make me a gift of yourself? Dare I, a sinner, appear before you? And do you forget your greatness and come to a sinner? You know this servant of yours; you know nothing good of him, to make him deserve this gift at your hands. I do not hide my wretchedness; I acknowledge your goodness, I praise your kindness, I thank you for your overwhelming love. It is for your own sake that you do this, not for any merit of mine. It is to make your goodness better known to me, to bestow your love more fully upon me, to give me a more wondrous example of humility. Since, then, it pleases you so to deal with me, since you have commanded that things should be so, it pleases me in my turn that you should so stoop to my lowliness; and I hope that my sinfulness may not stand as a barrier between us.

92

O Jesus, sweetest, kindest, what great worship and thanksgiving we ought to shew you, what never-ending praise, in return for the gift of your holy body! There is not a man to be found able to unfold in words its wonderful power. But what shall my thoughts be of as I make this Communion of mine, as I draw near to my Lord? To worship him as I ought is beyond my power, and yet I long to receive him devoutly.

What better thought can I have, what thought more profitable for my soul's health, than this: to abase myself entirely before you and to praise your boundless goodness towards me? I praise you, O my God, I give you glory for ever. Myself I look on with scorn and place at your feet, in the depths of my nothingness.

93

Look, Lord, you are the Saint of all Saints, and I but a filthy sinner; you bend down to me, because I am not worthy to lift my gaze towards you. Yes, you come to me; you want to be with me; you invite me to your feast. You wish to give me heavenly food to eat, the *Bread of Angels*[5]: your own self, no less, that living bread which came down from heaven and gives life to the world.

94

See where love has its source, see how brightly shines this divine abasement! How deep should our thanks be, how sincere our praise, for this your gift. It was indeed a device to heal and profit our souls, when you brought this Sacrament into being; a sweet and joyous banquet indeed, in which you gave yourself to be our food. What wonderful things you do, Lord! How mighty your power is, how unfailing your truth! You gave the word, and everything came into being; so was it with this Sacrament, because it was you who so gave command.

95

How wonderful a thing it is, worthy of man's belief, yet exceeding the grasp of his mind, that you, my Lord and my God, truly God and truly man, are wholly contained beneath the lowly shape of bread and wine; that you are eaten by him who receives you, and yet not consumed. You, the Lord of all things, who stand in need of nothing, have wished to live in our midst by means of this Sacrament. Keep my heart and my body free from stain, so that with a glad and untroubled conscience I may take part more frequently in this mystery of yours; and may I receive to my eternal salvation this Sacrament that you have blessed and devised to be for your own particular honour, your everlasting keepsake.

96

Be glad, my soul; thank God for leaving behind for you in this vale of tears so precious a gift as this is, so matchless a comfort. For every time you consider this mystery and receive the body of Christ you are furthering the work of your redemption and partaking in all the merits of Christ. There is never any lessening of the love Christ has for us, never a running dry of the stream of his pitiful intercession on our behalf. What you ought to do, then, is to prepare yourself each time for this Sacrament by thinking of it afresh, by pondering with careful consideration the great mystery of salvation. Whenever you say Mass or hear it, it ought to seem to you as great, as unexpected and as joyful a thing as if that same day Christ had first come down into the Virgin's womb and become man; as if he were hanging on the cross, suffering and dying for the salvation of men.

ON THE ADVANTAGE OF FREQUENT COMMUNION

97

Look, Lord, I have come to you here to benefit from your gift, to be gladdened by that holy feast of yours, that feast which in your kindness you have made ready for the poor, O my God. In you is everything that I can or should desire; you are my salvation and my redemption, my hope and my strength, my honour and my glory. Then comfort today *your servant's heart, this heart that aspires to you*, Lord Jesus.[6] I long now to receive you with devotion and reverence; I would fain shew you into my home. So may I deserve, like Zaccheus of old, to win your blessing and to be assigned a place among the children of Abraham. My soul longs for your body; my heart is athirst to become one with you.

98

Give me yourself—that is all I want; apart from you there is nothing able to bring me comfort. Without you I cannot exist; without these visits of yours I cannot live. That is why I must often approach you and receive you as medicine that brings health to my soul; if not, I shall faint by the wayside, deprived of this heavenly food. Yours is a heart overflowing with pity, my Jesus; when you were preaching to the people and healing their manifold diseases, you said once: *I must not send them away fasting, or perhaps they will grow faint on their journey.*[7] So deal with me as you did with them; it was to comfort those faithful to you that you left your presence behind in this Sacrament. You are the soul's sweet refreshment; the man who receives you worthily will share by inheritance the everlasting glory. But how often I slip into sin; how quickly I grow dull of heart and neglectful! That is why it is vital for me to freshen myself, to clean myself, to stir the fire in my heart by frequent prayer and confession. If I neglect these means too long, I may fall away from my good resolutions.

99

A man's senses have a twist towards evil from his youth upward; without the help of this divine medicine, he soon starts slipping into bigger sins. It is Holy Communion that drags him away from evil and gives him strength to remain good. I am often careless and lukewarm now, when I say Mass or go to Communion; what would it be like if I didn't take this remedy, if I neglected to seek the great help it gives me? I may not be fit to say Mass every day, may not be in the right dispositions; but I will make it my business to receive the divine mysteries at suitable times and make ready to share in the great grace they bestow. This is the chief comfort of the faithful soul, all the time it is journeying apart from you in this mortal body: oftentimes to remember its God and with devout heart to welcome her Beloved within her.

100

Lord God, you who give being and life to all souls, how wonderful is the way in which your love stoops to our lowliness! You do not think it below you to come to a poor, unworthy soul and to appease her hunger with the fullness of your Godhead and your manhood alike! Happy the mind, blessed the soul, that deserves reverently to receive you, her Lord and her God, and in receiving you to be filled with spiritual gladness! How great a Lord is he whom she receives, how beloved a guest; how pleasant a companion, how faithful a friend! How beauteous and noble a spouse she embraces, one that surpasses all other loves, one to be loved more than all that tempts our desire. O my beloved, my most sweet Jesus, let heaven and earth fall silent before you, with all their lovely adornment; whatever they have that makes us praise and admire them is but granted to them by your unstinting kindness; they fall far short of the beauty of your name, you whose wisdom is beyond all reckoning.

ON THE MANY BENEFITS ACCORDED TO THOSE WHO COMMUNICATE DEVOUTLY

101

O Lord my God, so guide this servant of yours with the blessings of your kindness that I may deserve to approach this your Sacrament with due devotion. Stir up my heart to meet you; strip from me the sloth that weighs upon me. Visit me with your healing presence; let me taste in spirit that sweetness of yours which, as in a fountain, gushes unseen in this Sacrament. Give light to my eyes; enable me to gaze on this great mystery. Give me strength to believe it with unwavering faith. What takes place is your doing; it is brought about by no power of man. It is your own holy institution, not something man has invented. Nowhere will you find a man capable by himself of grasping and understanding these things; they elude even the fine intelligence of the Angels. Then what about me, who am an unworthy sinner, nothing but dust and ashes? How can I examine, how grasp so deep, so holy a mystery?

102

Lord, with honesty of intent, with firm good faith and at your bidding I come to you full of hope and adoration; I really do believe you are present here in this Sacrament, both God and man. It is your wish that I should receive you, to become one with you in love. It is for this that I beg for your mercy, earnestly asking you to give me a special grace; let me dissolve and be one with you; let me overflow with your love; let me henceforth allow entrance to no comfort but such as comes from you. This most high and adorable Sacrament is the health of body and soul, the remedy for every spiritual disease. By it my vices are cured, my passions bridled, my temptations overcome or diminished;

grace is poured out more lavishly in my soul, budding virtue made to bloom, faith made firm, hope strengthened and love set afire and spread abroad.

103

O my God, keeper of my soul, restorer of human frailty and giver of all inward consolation, many are the blessings you have showered in this Sacrament, many and frequent the blessings you shower still on the souls you love when they make a devout Communion. Great is the comfort you give them against all sorts of trouble; from the depths of their despondency you lift them up and give them hope in your protection; and with fresh grace you cheer and enlighten their hearts. Thus it is that those who before Communion felt distressed and lacking in love find themselves afterwards changed for the better, now that they have been refreshed by that heavenly meat and drink.

In so dealing with your chosen you have a purpose. It is to make them conscious of the truth, by their own plain experience, that by themselves they are extremely weak, and that from you they gain an immense store of goodness and grace. They learn that by themselves they are cold, hardhearted and lacking in devotion, but after receiving you they gain in fervour, eagerness and devout affection. Who that comes humbly to the fountain of sweetness does not take away with him a little of its sweetness? Who can stand by a roaring fire and not feel something of its heat? And you are a fountain ever brimming and overflowing, a fire perpetually burning and never extinguished.

104

So, then, if I may not draw from the fullness of this fountain, may not drink till my thirst is utterly slaked, yet will I put my mouth to a hole in this heavenly pipe; so may I catch from it a tiny drop to allay my thirst and prevent my being parched within.

If I cannot yet become a creature of heaven, aflame with love, like the Cherubim and Seraphim, I will at least try to be earnest at my devotions and make ready my heart, so that by humbly receiving this life-giving Sacrament I may catch a spark, be it never so little, of the divine fire. O good Jesus, O most holy Saviour, do you of your kindness and grace make up for me whatever in me may be wanting; for you did not disdain to call all men to you, when you said: *Come to me, all you that labour and are burdened; I will give you rest.*

105

Labour? Yes, I labour in the sweat of my brow; I am tormented by anguish of heart, weighed down by my sins, troubled by temptations, entangled and oppressed by many an evil passion. There is no one to help me, no one to bring me to freedom and safety but you, Lord God, my Saviour. To you I entrust myself and all that is mine, that you may keep me and bring me to life everlasting. Take me, for the praise and glory of your name, you who have given me your body and your blood to be my meat and drink. Grant, O Lord God my Saviour, that through often receiving your mysteries my sense of devotion may grow ever greater.

ON THE DEEP REVERENCE WITH WHICH CHRIST IS TO BE RECEIVED

106

O Christ, the everlasting Truth, all these are sayings of yours, although they were not all spoken on one occasion or written down in a single passage. Since, then, they are yours, and since they are true, it is for me to welcome them all with faith and gratitude. Your sayings they are; it was you who spoke them; mine, too, because it was for my salvation that you uttered them. Gladly do I take them from your lips, that they may be implanted all the more firmly in my heart. So kindly those words of yours are, so full of sweetness and love, they stir my soul; but my own sins fill me with fear, my troubled conscience flails me when I would receive so great a mystery. The sweetness of your words calls me on, but my clustering sins weigh me down.

107

You bid me approach you in faith, if I would share what is yours; to receive the food of immortality, if I desire to win glory and life everlasting. *Come to me*, you say, *all you that labour and are burdened; I will give you rest*. O Lord, my God, how sweet and friendly do those words sound in the ear of a sinner! those words in which you invite the poor and the needy to the Communion of your most holy body! But, Lord, who am I to dare approach you? Why, the heaven of heavens cannot contain you; and yet you say, "Come to me, all of you".

108

What is the meaning of so loving a disregard of your dignity, so friendly an invitation? How shall I dare come? I know of no good in me that might give me grounds so to presume. How shall I bring you into my home, I who so many a time have wronged your immense kindness to me? Angel and Archangels bow down before you, Saints and holy people stand in dread of you; and yet you say, "Come to me, all of you".

If it were not you, Lord, saying these words, who would believe them? If it were not your own command, who would dare draw near?

109

That good man Noe toiled for a hundred years, building the ark, that he and a few besides might be saved; then how shall I, in a single hour, fit myself to receive with proper respect the creator of the world? Your great servant Moses, that special friend of yours, made an ark of imperishable wood, decking it with the finest gold, in order to place the Tablets of the Law inside; and shall I, perishable creature that I am, dare so easily to receive you, the framer of the law, the giver of life? Solomon, wisest of the kings of Israel, gave seven years to building a magnificent temple in praise of your name; for eight days he kept the feast of its dedication; a thousand victims he sacrificed as peace-offerings, and amid joyous applause and the braying of trumpets he solemnly took the ark of the covenant to the place made ready for it: and shall I, poorest and most wretched of men, bring you into my home, I who know how to spend scarce half an hour devoutly? I wish I could spend even half an hour as it ought to be spent!

110

Ah, my God, how much did those men strive to do to win your regard! And how little it is that I do; how short a time I take in preparing to make my Communion! Rarely am I completely recollected; rarely indeed am I entirely free from distraction. In the saving presence of your Godhead, no unseemly thought should arise, nothing created should take hold of my mind; for he who is to enter the guest-room of my heart is not an Angel, but the Angels' very Lord.

111

And yet how great a difference there is between the ark of the covenant and its relics, and your spotless body and its mighty powers, powers that beggar speech; between those sacrifices of the Old Law, the pattern of that which was to come, and the true victim of your body, the fulfilment of those sacrifices of old.

112

Then why is my heart not more aflame at your wondrous presence? Why don't I take greater care in preparing to receive your holy gift, seeing that those holy patriarchs and prophets of old, those kings and princes, together with all their people, shewed such great devotion for divine worship?

113

David, that most devout of kings, danced with all his might before the ark of God, when he recalled the kindnesses bestowed of old upon his forefathers; he devised all sorts of musical instruments and wrote psalms, which he taught his people to sing with gladness; he himself, too, often sang to the harp, when moved by the grace of the Holy Spirit. He taught the people of Israel to praise God with all their heart, to join each day in blessing him and telling of his goodness. If people in those days performed such acts of devotion, recalling the praise of God before the ark of the covenant, how great today should be the homage and devotion paid by me and by all Christian people in the presence of the Blessed Sacrament, and in receiving the most worshipful body of Christ?

114

There are many people who run off to various places to see relics of Saints; filled with wonder on hearing of their deeds, they look over the vast churches enshrining them and kiss the holy bones in their setting of silk and gold; and here you are before me on the altar, you, my God, the Saint of Saints, the maker of men, the Lord of the Angels. When men go to see such things it is often out of curiosity and a wish for change of scenery; they come back little inclined to amend their lives, especially when their pilgrimage has been a mere light-hearted dashing hither and thither, without any real touching of the heart. But here in the Sacrament of the altar you, my God, are wholly present, you, the man Christ Jesus. There we are dowered in abundance with the fruit of eternal salvation, every time that we receive you worthily and devoutly it is not frivolity that draws us there, not curiosity, not a desire for sensual pleasure, but firm faith, devout hope and love unfeigned.

115

How wonderful are your ways with us, O God, unseen maker of the world! How sweet and gracious your dealings with your chosen, when you offer yourself to them to be received in this Sacrament! It goes beyond all that the understanding can grasp; for devout souls it has a unique attraction, kindling in them the flames of love. Those who are truly faithful to you, who spend the whole of their lives trying to mend their faults, receive from this most adorable Sacrament the grace of devotion and the love of virtue.

116

Wonderful indeed is the grace that comes from this Sacrament, wonderful and hidden. It is only the faithful followers of Christ that know it; those who have no faith, those who are the slaves of sin, can have no conception of it. In this Sacrament we receive the gift of spiritual grace; the soul's lost strength is renewed, and the beauty that sin had marred returns to it once more. Indeed, so powerful is the grace of this Sacrament, so full the outpouring of devotion, that sometimes not only the mind but even the feeble body is aware that greater strength has been given it.

117

How great a pity it is, how much a matter for regret, that we are so lukewarm, so careless; that we are not drawn to receive Christ with greater love. For in him lies all the hope, all the merit, of those who are to be saved. It is he who makes us holy, he who redeems us; he who comforts us on our earthly journey, he who is the everlasting bliss of the Saints. Yes, a great pity it is that many have such scant regard for this saving mystery, which fills heaven with joy and keeps the whole creation in being. How blind men are, how hard their hearts, not to pay greater attention to so wondrous a gift as this! It even happens that their daily Communions become a mere formal routine.

118

Suppose that this most holy Sacrament were celebrated in one place only; suppose there were only one priest in the whole world to say the words of consecration. How men would long to go to that place, to visit that one priest of God and see the divine mysteries celebrated! But now there are many priests, and in many places Christ is offered, so that the further afield Holy Communion is spread throughout the world, the greater proof it may yield of God's grace and love for men. Thank you, O good Jesus, eternal shepherd, for deigning to refresh us poor outcasts with your precious body and blood; for inviting us with your own lips to partake of this mystery, when you say: *Come to me, all you that labour and are burdened; I will give you rest.*

ON THE CORRUPTION OF NATURE, AND THE POWER OF GOD'S GRACE

119

Lord Jesus, your life upon earth was known to but few, and the world sneered at it; grant that I may be like you in bearing the world's scorn; *a disciple is no better than his master, a servant than his lord.*[59] Let this servant of yours make your life his constant study; it is there that I find my salvation, and real holiness. Anything else that I read or hear of can neither feed my soul nor delight me so fully.

120

Lord Jesus, let what you have said and promised come true for me; let me earn what you have promised. I have taken the cross, look, taken it from your hands; I will carry it as you have laid it upon me, carry it until death. The life of a good monk is indeed a cross, but it leads him to heaven. We have made a start; we may not go back now, must not desert.

121

So come on, brothers, let us advance together; Jesus will be with us. It is for the sake of Jesus that we have taken up this cross; for his sake let us keep on with it to the end. He will help us, for he has gone before us to be our guide. See where that King of ours goes forth in front of us; he will be fighting at our side. Let us be men, and follow him, and none of us skulk in terror; let us be ready to die bravely in battle, and not sully our glory by abandoning the standard of the cross.